Maryland Historical Society

Report of the Committee on the Western Boundary of

Maryland

A Paper Read Before the Maryland Historical Society, December 9th, 1889

Maryland Historical Society

Report of the Committee on the Western Boundary of Maryland
A Paper Read Before the Maryland Historical Society, December 9th, 1889

ISBN/EAN: 9783337202842

Printed in Europe, USA, Canada, Australia, Japan

Cover: Foto ©ninafisch / pixelio.de

More available books at **www.hansebooks.com**

𝔉und-𝔓ublication, 𝔑o. 29.

REPORT OF THE COMMITTEE

ON THE

WESTERN BOUNDARY OF MARYLAND.

A Paper read before the Maryland Historical Society,

December 9th, 1889.

Baltimore. 1890.

PEABODY PUBLICATION FUND.

COMMITTEE ON PUBLICATION.

1889-90.

PRINTED BY JOHN MURPHY & CO.
PRINTERS TO THE MARYLAND HISTORICAL SOCIETY.
BALTIMORE, 1890.

REPORT.

THE original boundaries of the Province of Maryland were laid down with unwonted precision in the charter which created it. These were: the fortieth parallel of north latitude; a meridian line running south to the first or most distant fountain of the Potomac — ("ad verum meridianum primi fontis fluminis de Patowomack") thence proceeding southward (" deinde vergendo versus meridiem ") to the farther or western bank of that river, and following that bank to a specified point at the mouth of the river where it debouches into the Chesapeake: thence by a straight line across the bay to Watkins Point and onward to the ocean, and thence by the ocean and Delaware bay and river to the fortieth parallel.

Md. Charter in Md. Arch. Council, 1636–67. Appendix A.

The only one of these courses that was at all uncertain at the time the charter was granted, was that at the extreme west. The country to the west of the Alleghanies was then altogether unknown.

2

Indeed, for many years the geography of the continent was so little understood, that Herman, in his map (1670), considers the mountains about Cumberland to be the central ridge between the two oceans. The point at which the meridian line was to begin had, therefore, to remain undetermined until it should be found which was the furthest source or first fountain of the Potomac: in other words, which of the branches of that river took its rise farthest from its mouth. This point settled, the spring-head or source of that branch determined the western boundary of Maryland.

In 1649, Charles II, then a fugitive in Holland, granted to Lord Hopton, Sir Thomas Culpeper, and other exiled royalists, a tract of land in Virginia, lying between the rivers Rappahannock and Potomac, and running down to the Chesapeake Bay. Under the commonwealth, this remained, of course, a mere grant on paper; but after the restoration the grantees, or rather their heirs and assigns, proposed to avail themselves of their rights. Certain questions having been raised as to the validity of the original grant, these claimants surrendered their patent, and in 1669 received a re-grant, under the privy seal, of the lands in question. This grant, however, conveyed only a title to the soil, which still remained a part of Virginia, and subject to her

(marginal notes:) Boundary Com. Rep. 85. | Md. Acts, 1832. | Res. 128.

jurisdiction. It was not an enlargement of the territory of Virginia, but a grant within Virginia, and necessarily limited by the boundaries of that colony.

The Virginians were violently opposed to this grant, which placed the ownership of a vast extent of territory within two or three hands; and in 1675 they sent agents to England to remonstrate against it, or, if remonstrance were unavailing, to buy out the grantees' claims; but without success in either case. *McMahon, Hist. Md., p. 50.*

By the year 1688 the whole title had vested in Thomas, Lord Culpeper; and James II granted him a new patent for the whole tract. This descended to Catharine, his daughter and heiress, who brought it in marriage to Thomas, fifth Baron Fairfax of Cameron, in the Scottish peerage. Lord Fairfax proposed to reap some advantage from his immense territorial possessions, which were still unsurveyed; and in 1733 petitioned the King for the determination of his boundaries by commissioners. The petition was granted, and six commissioners were appointed, three representing Virginia, and three the Crown, who determined the boundaries separating his grant from the rest of Virginia. The grants had all called for lands lying south of the Potomac river; and consequently there was nothing in them interfering with the *Va. Acts, 1736.*

rights of Maryland. For this reason, probably, Charles, Lord Baltimore, made no attempt to have Maryland represented on the Commission. But when the question arose, which was the Potomac river, or which of the two great branches which unite to form it was the longer, the com-missioners (in 1736) concluded that the North Branch was the longer; Maryland, whose territory was at stake, having no voice in the matter.

Dinwiddie Papers, II, 351.

In 1745, Thomas, sixth Baron Fairfax, came to America; and on October 17, in the following year, surveyors engaged to run the line in conformity with the report of the commissioners. planted "the Fairfax Stone" to mark the northwestern limit of his grant. In 1748 the Virginia Assembly approved the line run by the commissioners, it was confirmed by the King in Council, and Fairfax opened an office for the sale of lands.

Ibid., I, 19. Faulkner's Report.

News of these proceedings reached Frederick, Lord Baltimore, and in his first letter of instructions (1753) to his new governor, Horatio Sharpe, he protests against this invasion of his territory, and directs the Governor to look into the matter, and to open correspondence with Lord Fairfax with a view to a settlement of boundaries between them.

Md. Archives, (MS.) Lib. J. R., U. S., p. 11. See Appen-dix B.

When these instructions were laid before the **Maryland Council**, they proceeded to inform themselves about the lands in question and the length of the rivers. They called before them Col. Thomas Cresap, a settler in the extreme west of the Province, who knew the country well; and he assured them that the South was the longer Ibid., p. 13. branch, running, as he believed, about sixty miles northwest farther than the North Branch.

Sharpe also wrote to Fairfax, calling his attention to the fact that the South Branch, according to the best information, was the true source of the Potomac, and proposing that they should unite in determining the correct boundary. Fairfax replied that he was of opinion that it would be to his advantage to have the South rather than the North Branch as his boundary: but that he thought the two governors were the proper persons to settle the question. He apparently believed that what he should gain by the extension of his territory to the west would more than offset what he should lose between the two branches. Colonel Cresap, in the next year, made a survey of both branches, and sent Governor Sharpe a map of his drawing, in which their position and length are pretty accurately laid down. A copy of this map is appended to this report.

Md. Arch. Sharpe Correspondence, I, 6, 7. See Appendix C.

Sharpe, Corr. I, 72.

Appendix D.

Sharpe. it is evident, was prepared to take all necessary steps for asserting and securing the rights of Maryland; but the outbreak of the French and Indian war in the next year (1754) prevented further action. We find him writing to the Proprietary in 1756 that " no survey can be safely made within eighty miles of the South Branch by less than a body of 100 or 200 men."

Sharpe,
Corr.,
I, 452.

In 1762 Colonel Cresap wrote in person to the Proprietary confirming his previous statements and adding particulars.

Md. Arch-
ives. MS.
Calvert
Pap's.

The treaty of Paris. in 1763, which closed the war, gave an opportunity for a final settlement of the question ; but the King, finding it necessary to adjust the boundaries of his colonial possessions, and to carry out his agreement with the Indians, issued a proclamation prohibiting the colonial governments from granting any lands lying west of the heads of rivers flowing into the Atlantic from the west and north-west. About the same time the Proprietary conceived the idea of reserving for himself a manor of 10,000 acres in the western part of the Province, and sent out orders that no lands beyond Cumberland were to be granted to settlers until this manor was laid off. These causes combined to prevent settlements in the extreme west of Mary-

Md. Arch.
MS.
Lib. J. R. &
U. S.,
p. 379-80.
Appendix
E.

land, which otherwise would have led to a final settlement of the boundary. Governor Eden, however, in 1771 appointed commissioners, of whom Cresap was one, to survey and mark the head of the South Branch. He did so; marked the spot with a stone bearing the letters CLDB, and continued the line northward. On completing his labors, he filed a very accurate map in the Land Office. Pigman's Rep., 1834.

In May, 1774, Mr. Jenifer, the Proprietary's agent, remonstrated against the action of the Board of Revenue, who were opening to settlers the lands of the "Western Reserve," as it was called, telling the Board that while there was no doubt that the South Branch was the true boundary of the Province, yet that it was inexpedient to grant lands in the territory claimed by Fairfax while the Proprietary was waiting an opportunity to bring the whole matter before the King. The Board reply that it is not for them to take any action which may tend to prejudice the Proprietary's claims or imply any doubt as to their validity. "The Proprietary," they say, "has lately been at the expense of running a line to the South Branch; and if the Virginians hear that he doubts about the extension of these limits, it will be an encouragement to them to begin to throw stones." Holding this view, they continued to Proc. Bd. of Revenue. McMahon.

grant lands in the Western Reserve until October, 1774, when instructions were received from the guardians of the new Proprietary, Henry Harford (a minor), to suspend all further grants of the reserved lands.

Thus the question stood at the outbreak of the Revolution. Fairfax still held the northern neck under the royal government of Virginia; and when that colony assumed the position of a sovereign State, he held it under the State government. In 1785, on account of the alienage of Denny Fairfax, McMahon, devisee of Lord Fairfax, the Virginia p. 59. Assembly claimed the land as forfeit; but this claim was not upheld by the Supreme 1813, Court of the United States.
7th Cranch, 607. At the outbreak of the Revolution, (McMahon.) then, the question was still unsettled. Maryland claimed her western boundary under her charter, which had never been revoked or broken; and this claim had never been yielded, waived, or compromised. This claim, from the first, was to the farthest source of the Potomac, whichever that might be found to be; and undisputed surveys had shown that the South Branch took its rise from the farthest source, and was therefore the true boundary of Maryland.

Virginia recognized the equity of Maryland's position, and in her first Constitution, adopted June 29, 1776, inserted an article confirming to the

State of Maryland, in the fullest and most explicit manner, all that the latter claimed. The words are:

"The territories contained within the charters erecting the colonies of Maryland, Pennsylvania, North and South Carolina, are hereby ceded, released, and forever confirmed to the people of those colonies respectively, with all the rights of property, jurisdiction, and government, and all other rights whatsoever which might, at any time heretofore, have been claimed by Virginia, except the free navigation and use of the rivers Potomac and Pokomoke, with the property of the Virginia shores or strands bordering on either of the said rivers, and all improvements which have been or shall be made thereon." Va. Const., 1776, Art. 21.

Though this was full and complete enough, yet the phraseology " ceded " and " released " implied an assertion of rights which Maryland had never admitted. The first Constitutional Convention of Maryland (October, 1776) was by no means disposed to allow the State to be represented as the recipient of Virginia's bounty ; and in order that her position and claims might be perfectly clear, this article of the Virginia constitution was taken into consideration, and the following resolution adopted :

" Resolved, unanimously, that it is the opinion of this Convention that the State of Virginia hath not any right or title to any of the territory, bays, rivers, or waters included in the charter granted by his majesty, Charles I, to Cecilius Calvert, Baron of Baltimore." Jour. of Convention.

14

After this disclaimer on the part of Virginia and assertion of rights by Maryland, a compact was made between the two States, Messrs. Jenifer, Stone, and Chase being the commissioners on the part of Maryland, and Mason and Henderson on the part of Virginia, providing for riparian rights on the Potomac, trespasses, the return of fugitives from justice, etc. This compact was ratified by the legislatures of both states in the same year, and re-enacted in the Virginia codes of 1849 and 1860.

So careful was Maryland, on the one hand, not to seem to waive any of her rights, and, on the other, not to appear discourteous to Virginia, who appeared so equitably disposed to her, that when, in 1788, it became necessary to allot portions of the Western Reserve as bounty-lands to soldiers of the Revolution, care was taken to set out the 2575 allotments in territory north of the North Branch of the Potomac, and running next to "the present supposed boundary of Maryland." Under a resolution of the Assembly in the previous year, Francis Deakin had been employed to survey and plot the lands lying west of Fort Cumberland, and by his plot the bounty-lands were laid out. But to avoid all misconstruction, in the same act the Assembly declared:

Hening, XII, 50. Md. Acts, 1785, Ch. I, (Kilty.)

Md. Acts (Kilty) 1788, Ch. 44.

Md. Acts, 1788, Ch. 44. Preamble.

15

" That the line to which the said Francis Deakin has laid out the said lots is, in the opinion of the General Assembly, far within that which this State may rightfully claim as its western boundary ; and that at a time of more leisure the consideration of the legislature ought to be drawn to the western boundaries of this State, as objects of very great importance."
§ 15.

As the Charter of Maryland was clear in the definition of the boundary, and as the Constitution of Virginia had pledged that State to acceptance of the line laid down in the Charter, nothing now remained to be done but to survey and mark the line. In 1795, by a resolution of the Assembly, Messrs. Pinkney, Cooke, and Key were appointed commissioners on the part of Maryland to meet a commission from Virginia, and adjust the southern and western boundaries of the State. Mr. Pinkney, however, was sent on a foreign mission, and Mr. Cooke declined to act, as did also Messrs. Carroll and Chase, who were appointed in their places. Mr. Key soon afterwards removed from the State.
Vid. Md. Acts, 1831. Res. 128.

In 1801 the Assembly, by a resolution, empowered the Governor and Council to appoint commissioners for the same purpose, and Messrs. Duvall, McDowell, and Nelson were appointed on the part of Maryland. Part of the
Md. Acts, ut supra.

correspondence between Governors Mercer and Monroe has been preserved. from which it appears that the Virginia legislature appointed commissioners, but limited their powers to a settlement of the western line.

Council Rec., 1802, Jun. & Nov. (See McMahon.)

In this correspondence Gov. Mercer points out that the first step to be taken is to determine on which of the branches the first fountain of the Potomac is to be found. This point once settled, there could be no possibility of dispute as to the western boundary, which was a due north line from that point; nor as to the south-western boundary, which followed the right bank of the river. This disagreement seems to have prevented further proceedings; and though, in 1803, Governor Mercer, then in the Maryland House of Delegates, recommended running a provisional line until further steps could be taken. nothing came of it. A resolution of similar tenor was passed in 1810, but without results.

Md. Acts, 1810. Res. 3.

By the year 1818. Maryland seems to have grown weary of attempts to recover her invaded territory, and the Assembly passed an Act authorizing the appointment of three commissioners to meet commissioners from Virginia, and run a line from "the most western source of the North Branch of the Potomac." due north to the Pennsylvania line. Foreseeing that even this

Md. Acts, 1818. Ch. 206.

line would inclose lands granted by Virginia, the
act provided for the regranting such lands free of
charge. This act, however, was not to be operative
until the Virginia legislature should have passed
an act with similar provisions. Virginia did not
act in the matter until 1821, when her legislature
passed an act indeed, but one differing materially
from the Maryland act. The Maryland act provided for the ascertainment of " the most western
source of the North Branch of the Potomac" as the
beginning of the line; the Virginia act   See
provided for the beginning of the line at   Md. Acts, 1831.
the Fairfax stone, which had never been   Res. 125.
recognized by Maryland, and, in fact, does not
mark the farthest source of even the North Branch.

Commissioners were, however, appointed by both
States: but on their meeting, in 1824, the Virginians
produced their instructions, which, in themselves,
were of a character to bar all further proceedings.
The Maryland act, as has been said, instructed her
commissioners to ascertain the most western source
of the North Branch, and begin the line there;
while the Virginia commissioners were instructed
to proceed to the Fairfax stone and begin the line
there. In other words, the compromise (if we can
call so one-sided an offer a compromise) which
Maryland, much to her own injury, had offered,
was not enough unless she would concede all that
Virginia now chose to claim. The Maryland com-

18

missioners were not willing, nor had they the power, to make this concession; while on the other hand the Virginians refused, or were not authorized, even to investigate the pretensions of the Fairfax stone to mark the farthest source of the North Branch. The line must begin where Virginia wanted it to begin, or not at all. So all negotiation came to nothing, and the act of 1818 was repealed in 1825. Maryland's offer of a compromise having been thus rejected, she was remitted to her original rights.

Boyle'sRep.
Md. Acts,
1824–5.
Ch. 195.

In 1826 resolutions were again passed by the Maryland Assembly providing for the appointment of commissioners to meet commissioners from Virginia and settle the boundary. In case of disagreement, the Governor of Delaware was to be requested to appoint an umpire. This resolution was not to go into effect until the Virginia Assembly should have provided for a similar commission, and should have pledged the faith of the State to abide by its award. A correspondence between Governors Kent and Tyler followed, but nothing came of it.

Md. Acts,
1825–6.
Res. 82.

In 1832 the Maryland Assembly (probably stimulated by the very able discussion of the question by McMahon in his *History of Maryland*, published in the preceding year) appointed a committee to inquire and report—

Md. Acts,
1831,
Res. 126.

1. What were the true charter boundaries of the State.

2. Whether the southern and western boundaries as laid down in the charter ought not to be taken as the true boundaries.

3. What is the first fountain of the Potomac as called for by the charter.

4. Whether Virginia had at any time recognized the claim of Maryland to all the land included in the charter.

5. Whether any survey could be found determining the first fountain of the Potomac.

6. The nature of the boundary dispute, the steps that had already been taken therein, and what further action, in their judgment, should be taken by the State to have the matter finally adjusted.

The committee reported at length. In answer to the first question, they recite and explain the language of the charter. To the second they say that the southern and western bounds as laid down in the charter should be the present boundaries of Maryland, that State having done nothing to divest herself of her rights. They add that the territory claimed is estimated to amount to 462.480 acres. To the third, that the first fountain of the Potomac can easily be determined by survey. To the fourth, they cite the declaration of the Virginia Convention of 1776, and the resolution

Ibid., Res. 128.

in the Maryland Convention. To the fifth, they cite
Cresap's survey of 1771, on file in the Land Office.
In answer to the sixth, the committee review the
whole controversy in its various stages. They con-
clude by recommending a commission similar to
that provided for by the resolutions of 1826,

"to settle and adjust by mutual compact between the two
governments the southern and western limits of this State,
and the dividing and boundary lines between this State and
the Commonwealth of Virginia."

As before, the Governor of Delaware was to be
requested to appoint an umpire; and the action of
the Assembly was to have no effect until Virginia
had provided for a similar commission, and pledged
the faith of the State (as Maryland did), to abide
by its award.

In 1833 the Assembly of Virginia took action in
Va. Acts, the matter, but it was action of a peculiar
1833, Ch. 32. kind. No notice is taken of Maryland's
See Appen-
dix F. overtures nor of her previous attempts
to bring about a settlement: the act is worded
as if it were a spontaneous and independent move-
ment on Virginia's part. It provides for the
appointment of three commissioners on the part of
Virginia "to meet such commissioners as may be
appointed for the same purpose by the Commonwealth of Maryland, to settle and adjust . . .   the

western limits of this State, and the dividing and
boundary line between this State and the Commonwealth of Maryland, to commence at the Fairfax
stone, or at the first fountain of the Cohongoroota,
or North Branch of the Potomac."

Of course this action, besides being in a high
degree discourteous to Maryland, was altogether
different from the Maryland resolutions. The
latter provided for a settlement by mutual compact,
the commissioners to investigate and determine
where the true boundary lay; the Virginia act,
while preserving the phrase "mutual compact,"
dictates the place at which the line is to begin, and
empowers its commissioners only to meet commissioners from Maryland appointed " for the same
purpose," that is, to begin the line at the Fairfax
stone, or the head of the Cohongoroota. It is evident that no commissioners appointed under the
Maryland resolutions would have power to make
this concession; and, in fact, the resolutions themselves could not go into effect. Moreover, no
provision was made for umpirage in case of disagreement, nor was the faith of the State pledged
to abide by the award. It was, in fact, a rejection
—and a rude rejection—of Maryland's friendly
overtures. Indeed the Virginia Assembly evi-
dently anticipated such an interpretation, and
provided that in case Maryland appointed no com-

missioners, the line should be run by Virginia alone, in the way she wanted it.

This rebuff exhausted Maryland's patience. On March 14, 1834, the Assembly passed a temperately worded resolution expressing regret at the rejection of their advances, and instructing the attorney-general of the State to institute proceedings in the Supreme Court of the United States to procure a final adjustment of the southern and western boundaries; but providing that such suit should cease at any time, before final judgment, if Virginia would accept the overtures of 1832.

Md. Acts, 1833. Res. 80.

It seemed now at last that the question must be definitely settled, either by mutual agreement or by judicial decision. But the resources of Virginia were not yet exhausted. Governor Tazewell, of that State, in his message of 1834, adverted to the matter, saying that Maryland had misunderstood the Virginia Act of 1833: that it was really intended as an acceptance, and not a rejection of the Maryland overtures: but that Maryland having thought fit to assume a menacing attitude, it did not now comport with the dignity of Virginia to go into explanations. This message was not officially communicated to the Maryland Legislature, but reached them through the public press.

This adroit move was perfectly successful. The matter having been referred to by Governor Thomas, in his message, the special committee to whom the subject was referred, report that they see nothing in the matter now brought before them which calls for "any relaxation or change in the course deliberately determined upon at the last session;" and they wish it clearly understood that Maryland "seeks or desires nothing which is not hers of right; and it is necessary for her honor that in a controversy, however amicable, the terms of adjustment shall not be dictated to her." The committee then refer to the Virginia act of 1833, which they declare "not only not in accordance with, but directly repulsive of," the Maryland overtures, and "an undertaking, in truth, by one of the parties absolutely to settle and pronounce against the claim of the other."

Md. Acts, 1834. Res. 99.

But they add, that since they have learned from Governor Tazewell's message that Virginia is willing to agree to terms of adjustment, "if the door of explanation be not closed upon her," they will not, for their part, let "any strained punctilio" stand in the way of an amicable settlement; and they will repeal the resolution of March 14, 1834, direct the attorney general to discontinue proceedings under it, and now stand ready and desirous to settle the long-pending controversy by amicable negotiation.

They were left standing in this amiable attitude. Virginia made no further move.

The provisional line of 1787, or "Deakin's line," as it was called, had long done duty as a boundary; and as the State granted no lands beyond it, it came to be looked upon—despite the emphatic protest of the Assembly of 1788, as the true boundary line of the State. In process of time the marks became obliterated, and conflicts of title and litigation arose between the holders of Maryland and the holders of Virginia patents for lands in the debatable territory. So in May, 1852, the Maryland Legislature passed an act reciting these facts and requesting the Governor to open a correspondence with the Governor of Virginia about the matter; and authorizing him to appoint a commissioner, if the Legislature of Virginia would also appoint one, which joint commission should run and mark a line due north from the Fairfax Stone, which line, when ratified by both Legislatures, should be the boundary between the States.

Md. Acts,
1852.
Ch. 275.

As this was an offer to give up the whole matter in controversy, it looked as if the contention was about to be settled at last. Virginia responded by an act of similar tenor in the following year. This, however, was superseded by an act passed in 1857–8 of somewhat different scope. This provided for a joint commission to trace the southern boundary from Smith's Point to the Atlantic ocean, and the western boundary from the Fairfax Stone to the Pennsylvania line.

As the Maryland act of 1852 only empowered the settlement of the western boundary. Mr. T. J. Lee, the commissioner appointed under it, met Col. Angus W. McDonald, on the part of Virginia, to carry out his instructions. By application to the Federal government the services of an experienced engineer. Lieutenant N. Michler, were secured, and a line from the Fairfax Stone north to the Pennsylvania line was run and marked. This line, when ratified by both Legislatures, was to be the definite boundary.

Maryland proceeded to ratify Michler's line by an act passed March 6, 1860. Virginia, however, did not proceed to ratification. Md. Acts, 1860. Ch. 385. In the session of 1859–60 the Virginia Assembly passed two resolutions dealing with the subject. In the first they provided for the erection of suitable monuments to mark Va. Acts, 1859–60. Res. 15. Michler's line; and in the second they authorized the governor to send an agent to England to collect record and documentary evidence "tending to ascertain and establish the true lines of boundary between Virginia and the States of North Carolina. Tennessee and Maryland." From this it would appear that they considered the boundary question still open. At all events, the ratification required by the act was not given, and Maryland was once more remitted to her original rights, her charter boundary and its acceptance by the Virginia Constitutional Convention.

The outbreak of the war in 1861, and its results, changed the status of the question. The State of West Virginia was separated from Virginia, and in her boundaries (which were designated by county lines) were included those counties in which the disputed territory lies. It was with West Virginia, therefore, that the question would have to be settled.

The Legislature of West Virginia, at the session W. Va. of 1868, authorized the Governor to Acts, 1868. appoint a commission to ascertain the line Ch. 175. between West Virginia and Maryland, commencing at the Fairfax Stone, and running north to the Pennsylvania line, and to communicate with the Governor of Maryland, with the view of having a joint survey made. The reason of this action was the fact that Michler's line having been found more favorable to Maryland than the old provisional, or Deakin's line. West Virginia took the ground that as Virginia had never ratified Michler's line, West Virginia was bound to nothing, and the question was still open.

In 1884 the Maryland Assembly passed a resolution by which, after the statement that there was difficulty in ascertaining the exact location of Mason and Dixon's line, owing to the absence of marks, the members of Congress from Maryland are requested to use their influence to obtain an appropriation from the Federal government " for the purpose of re-surveying and locating the said Mason and Dixon's line by marking said Mason and Dixon's line with suitable stone monuments, with the letters M. and V. between the States of Maryland and Virginia, M. and P. between the States of Maryland and Pennsylvania, M. and D. between Maryland and Delaware, commencing at the Fairfax Stone at the head waters of the north branch of the Potomac, thence running northwardly with Mason and Dixon's line until it intersects the eastwardly line dividing the States of Pennsylvania and Maryland "—and so forth.

Md. Acts,
1884.
Res. 5.

As the action contemplated by this resolution was, on the face of it, impracticable, your Committee have not thought it necessary to investigate what further steps, if any, were taken in the matter.

In 1886 a resolution was passed in the Maryland Assembly to the effect that as Michler's line had not yet been adopted by West Virginia, the Governor of Maryland should be requested to bring the subject to the

Md. Acts,
1886.
Res. 5.

attention of the Governor of West Virginia, asking him to bring it before the Legislature of that State for such action as they might deem fitting.

In the next year the Assembly of West Virginia passed an act confirming Michler's line, but not unconditionally. The act was not to take effect until Maryland should have passed an act or acts confirming all Virginia patents to "lands situate .... between the new Maryland line hereby established, and the old Maryland line heretofore claimed by Virginia and West Virginia to the same extent and like legal effect as though the said old Maryland line were hereby confirmed and established."

W. Va. Acts, 1887. See Appendix G.

This clause introduces a new and important feature in the case. Michler's line differs considerably from the old line, running from the Fairfax Stone more to the westward, and giving to Maryland, as your Committee are informed, a wedge of territory three-quarters of a mile at the base, and thirty-seven miles long. All the lands within this wedge, your Committee are informed, are covered by grants from Virginia and a considerable part of them by grants from Maryland. Maryland is therefore called upon to annul her own grants and oust her own citizens from her own acknowledged territory as a condition of getting back a small fraction of the lands of which she has been despoiled.

In 1888 the question arose again in the Assembly of Maryland. On March 13, a resolution was passed in the Senate to the effect that whereas, while Maryland had ratified the Michler line of 1859, Virginia had never done so: and whereas Maryland had endeavored, without avail, to induce West Virginia to adopt it, or to settle the matter by a joint commission, that State had not complied,—that now the Attorney-General of the State be applied to, to advise the proper remedy.

Sen. Jour., 1888.

The Attorney-General replied (March 17) saying:

" In my judgment, no definite settlement of that matter can be accomplished by the appointment of Commissioners, or by negotiations between the Legislatures of the respective States. The controversy has been going on for more than a century, and the State of Maryland has appointed commission after commission to make such adjustment, but all to no purpose." . . .

" In my judgment, therefore, there are but two courses open to bring this long-pending controversy to an end. One is for the State to cause proceedings to be taken against the State of West Virginia in the Supreme Court of the United States for the purpose of procuring a final legal adjustment and settlement of the boundary line between the States ; and the other is to submit the matter in controversy to arbitrators appointed by the States."

He concluded by recommending the passage of an act providing for an arbitration, and submitted the draft of such an act.

The bill was introduced in the Senate on March 19, and referred to the Committee on Federal Relations.

We may infer that upon mature consideration it was judged inexpedient to entrust a decision of so much moment to the State to the judgment of a single man (since this is what an arbitration usually comes to), and when the bill providing for arbitration was reported back to the Senate, it was reconsidered, and the enacting clause stricken out.

Thus stands the question at the present moment. Nothing final has been done since the Virginia Convention of 1776, which acknowledged the right of Maryland to her charter-boundary, and waived all claims that Virginia might have made to any territory within it, incorporating these words, for the greater solemnity, in the Constitution of the State.

In conclusion, your committee beg to offer the following Resolutions:

RESOLVED, That, in the opinion of this Society, it is highly desirable that the true western boundary of Maryland which has been so long in dispute, should be equitably and finally determined; and this Society approves the view of the late John V. L. McMahon, that the best mode of settlement is by a decision of the Supreme Court of the United States.

RESOLVED, That a copy or copies of this report be transmitted to the members of the Hon. Legislature of Maryland at their next session.

All which is respectfully submitted.

WM. HAND BROWNE, } *Committee.*
ALBERT RITCHIE,

———

APPENDIX.

APPENDIX A.

" Totam illam partem peninsule sive chersonesus jacentem
Pat. Roll,
8, Charles I,
III,
2594.
in partibus Americe inter oceanum ex oriente et
sinum de Chessopeake ab occidente a residuo ejusdem per rectam lineam a promontorio sive capite
terre vocate Watkins Point juxta sinum predictum prope
fluvium de Wighco scituato ab occidente usque ad magnum
oceanum in plaga orientali ductam divisam et inter metam
illam a meridie usque ad partem illam estuarii de De la Ware
ab aquilone que subjacet quadragesimo gradui latitudinis sep-
tentrionalis ab equinoctiali ubi terminatur Nova Anglia totum-
que illius terre tractum infra metas subscriptas videlicet trans-
eundo a dicto estuario vocato Delaware Baye recta linea per
gradum predictum usque ad verum meridianum primi fontis
fluminis de Pattowomack deinde vergendo versus meridiem
ad ulteriorem dicti fluminis ripam et eam sequendo qua plaga
occidentalis et meridionalis spectat usque ad locum quendam
appellatum Cinquak prope ejusdem fluminis ostium scituatum
ubi in prefatum sinum de Chessopeak evolvitur ac inde per
lineam brevissimam usque ad predictum promontorium de
Watkins Point."

33

34

APPENDIX B.

From Frederick, Lord Baltimore's, Instructions to Gov. Horatio Sharpe, 1753.

" Whereas the Right Honorable Lord Viscount Fairfax has
a grant of a large tract of land lying and running
along the banks of Patowmack River on the Virginia side, and whereas I am informed the powers
of government in Virginia have taken the liberty
to ascertain the bounds and limits of his said Lordship's grant
running along the banks of the said river, which river, to the
further bank thereof, is limited to me with its soil and water,
and is a boundary between my Province of Maryland and the
Province of Virginia unto the fountain head of the said river;
and whereas I am informed that commissioners have proceeded therein, and instead of their stopping at South Branch,
which runs from the first fountain of Patowmack River, one
of the boundaries of Maryland, have crossed to a branch running north, whereby their endeavours are to give limits and
boundary marks prescribed by my royal charter, subjecting
me to great loss of country; and whereas it being not known
to me that my predecessor was made a party to the settlement
of such boundaries by the said commissioners; and were it so,
such settlement would be invalid by virtue of my father's
marriage-articles, he being only tenant for life, with reserva-
tion to me as tenant in tail; I therefore desire and require of
you, as soon as possibly you can, to get intelligence how such
boundaries have been or are settled by the said commissioners
with regard to Lord Fairfax and his grant; and at the same
time, if opportunity serves you, you may communicate to Lord
Fairfax that I am very desirous of settling proper limits con-

Md. Arch. MS. Lib., J.R.&U.S., p. 11.

clusive between him and me in regard to my Province of Maryland and his grant in Virginia; and in the mean time you must make or have made a good look out, and warning given to such persons as shall venture to settle in such disputed boundary between my Province of Maryland and the Province of Virginia under the said grant to Lord Fairfax."

APPENDIX C.

SHARPE TO FAIRFAX.

[Sept. 1753.]

" . . . . Lord Baltimore was pleased to charge me with an inquiry into the true meridian and place of the fountain head of Potowmack. The best information I have hitherto been able to procure gives me reason to believe there has been a mistake in fixing the spring head to the North Branch, since the length, with other circumstances, more properly denotes the Southern Branch, commonly called Wappacomo, to be the main and principal course of that river. I am the more willing to be persuaded of the truth of this representation from the considerable advantage that will accrue to your Lordship. That branch, I am informed, has never been thoroughly explored and traced to its source; but I flatter myself with having your Lordship's concurrence for such an examination into its course, length, width, and depth as may bring this matter to a nearer degree of certainty; and if that should appear to be the fountain head of Patowmeck River, I shall not question but your Lordship will be for taking such measures as may ascertain the mutual limits of the two Proprietorships, agreeable to the direction and true intention of their respective charters."

Md. Arch.
Sharpe Cor.
I., 6.

Fairfax to Sharpe.

"*Frederick*, Septemb᷄ the 24ᵗʰ, 1753.

"*Sir:* Yours I received by Mr. Young, by which I perceive Lord Baltimore designs to dispute with this Province which is the head spring of Patowmeck, the south or north branch as run out by the commissioners between his Majesty and me in the year 1736.

"I am intirely [of the opinion?] that the South would be much to my advantage, and therefore think it improper for me to appear therein, and that the Governor of Virginia and your excellency should transact that affair. If his Lordship should obtain his demand, I must insist upon a new line between his Majesty and me to the Southward."

———————

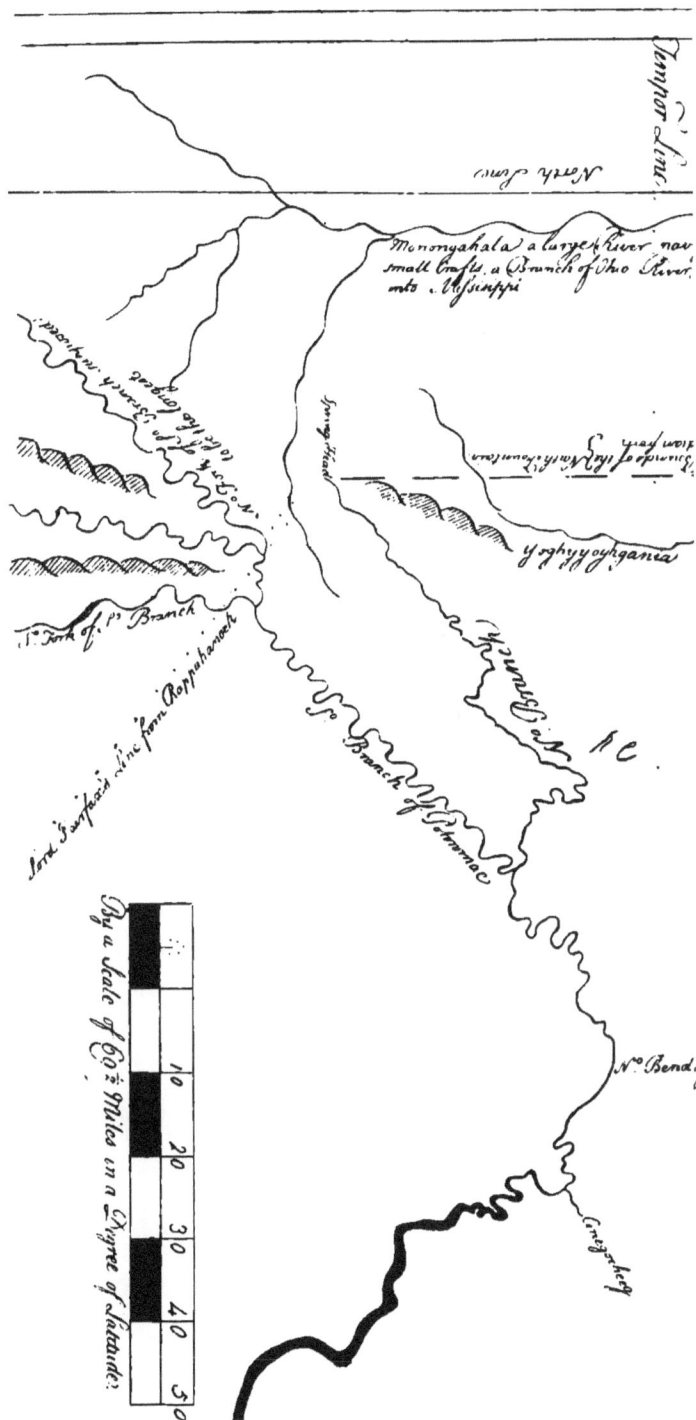

Temper Line.

North Line.

Monongahala a large River now
small Crafts, a Branch of Ohio River,
into Mississippi

Spring Head

Branch of this Mountain
y Branch of this Mountain

Yorghy yoyhganta

Ct B

1st Fork of Pr Branch

Branch of Potomac

Lord Fairfax's line from Rappahanock

No Bend.

Cumberland

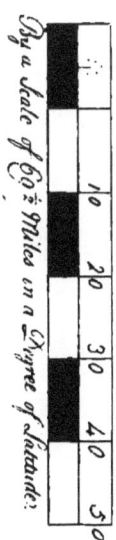

By a Scale of 69½ Miles on a Degree of Latitude.

10 20 30 40 50

APPENDIX E.

EXTRACT FROM THE ROYAL PROCLAMATION OF OCT. 7, 1763.

"And whereas it is just and reasonable, and essential to Our interest and the security of Our colonies that the several nations or tribes of Indians with whom We are connected, and who live under Our protection, should not be molested or disturbed in the possession of such parts of Our dominion and territories as, not having been ceded to, or purchased by, Us, are reserved to them or any of them, as their hunting-grounds, We do therefore, with the advice of Our Privy Council, declare it to be Our Royal will and pleasure that no Governor or Commander-in-Chief in any of Our Colonies of Quebec, East Florida, or West Florida, do presume, upon any pretense whatever, to grant warrants of survey or pass any patents for land beyond the bounds of their respective governments as described in their commissions; as also that no Governor or Commander-in-Chief in any of Our other Colonies or Plantations in America do presume for the present, and until Our further pleasure be known, to grant warrants of survey or pass patents for any lands beyond the heads or sources of any of the rivers which fall into the Atlantic ocean from the west and north-west."

Md. Arch. MS. Lib. J. R. & U. S. p. 379.

APPENDIX F.

Act passed March 5, 1833.

Commonwealth of Virginia.

Chap. 32. *An Act to settle the western limits of this State, and the dividing and boundary line between this State and the Commonwealth of Maryland.*

1. Be it Enacted *by the General Assembly of the Commonwealth of Virginia:*

That the Governor be, and he is hereby authorized, to appoint three Commissioners on the part of this State to meet such Commissioners as may be appointed for the same purpose by the Commonwealth of Maryland, to settle and adjust, by mutual compact between the two governments, the western limits of this State, and the dividing and boundary line between this State and the Commonwealth of Maryland, to commence at the Fairfax stone, or at the first fountain of the Cohongoroota or north branch of the Potomac river, and to run a due north course to intersect the line between this State and the State of Pennsylvania. If, however, the Commonwealth of Maryland shall fail to appoint Commissioners, then, and in that event, the commissioners appointed by the Governor of this Commonwealth, or any two of them, shall run and mark the said line according to the provisions of this bill: and the Commissioners appointed as aforesaid are required to report their proceedings in virtue of their appointment and authority to the General Assembly of this State at the session next after the same shall have been concluded, for confirmation or rejection.

[The remaining sections provide for re-granting lands "after the confirmation of the settlement as aforesaid;" for the employment of a surveyor and assistants and their payment, as also the payment of the commissioners; and that the act shall be in force from the time of its passage.]

APPENDIX G.

Acts West Virginia, 1887, Extra Session.

CHAPTER I. *An Act to confirm and establish a part of the boundary line between the State of W. Va. and the State of Md. (Passed May 3, 1887.)*

BE IT ENACTED *by the Legislature of West Virginia:*

1. That the boundary line as run and marked by N. Michler, U. S. engineer, in the year one thousand eight hundred and fifty-nine, under the direction of A. W. McDonald, Commissioner on the part of Virginia, and Thos. J. Lee, Commissioner on the part of Maryland, from the Fairfax Stone to the Pennsylvania line, between the county of Preston, W. Va., and the county of Alleghany, now Garrett, Maryland, be and the same is hereby approved and confirmed as the true boundary line between the State of West Virginia and the State of Maryland.

2. But this act shall not take effect until and unless the State of Maryland shall pass an act or acts confirming and rendering valid all entries, grants, patents and titles from the Commonwealth of Virginia, to any person or persons, to lands situate and lying between the new Maryland line hereby established and the old Maryland line heretofore claimed by Virginia and West Virginia, to the same extent and like legal effect, as though said old Maryland line were hereby confirmed and established.

Approved May 6th, 1887.

APPENDIX II.

NOTE ON FAULKNER'S REPORT.

An opinion having got abroad that Faulkner's report to the Governor of Virginia in 1832, was in some way decisive of this question, it may be as well to dispose of it here. It is probably traceable to a letter published by him in 1875, in which he says that the evidence he submitted had such "overwhelming" effect on the Legislature of Maryland, that they at once dismissed the suit in the Supreme Court and abandoned the claim.

Faulkner's report consists partly of well-known facts, sometimes incorrectly cited (for example he misquotes the Maryland Charter and founds a long argument on the misquotation); partly of documents relating to the adjustment of the bounds between Fairfax and Virginia, which have little bearing on the question at issue, and partly of his personal opinions on the matter, which have, if possible, less.

As matter of fact, the record shows as we have seen, that the Maryland Legislature, so far from being "overwhelmed," or abandoning any claim, reasserted the rights of the State, and declared that they saw nothing in the documents laid before them to induce them to vary from the course determined on. But, out of courtesy to Virginia, they would withdraw the suit, as they had learned from high quarters that that alone stood in the way of an amicable settlement, which was all they desired.